Melissa Feldman (left), Portia and Liza Colón-Zayas in a scene from the New York production of *Our Lady of 121st Street*.

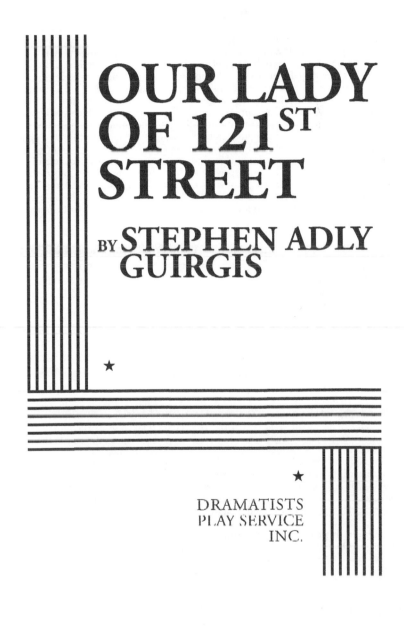

OUR LADY OF 121ST STREET

BY STEPHEN ADLY GUIRGIS

★

★

DRAMATISTS
PLAY SERVICE
INC.

2

For

Therese Cunningham Guirgis & KaDee Strickland

and in loving memory of

Juan Jose Ortiz (1943–2001)
R.I.P.

OUR LADY OF 121ST STREET was originally produced in New York City by LAByrinth Theater Company. It was subsequently produced Off-Broadway at the Union Square Theatre by John Gould Rubin, Ira Pittelman, Robyn Goodman, Ruth Hendel and Daryl Roth, opening on March 6, 2003. It was directed by Philip Seymour Hoffman; the assistant director was Brian Roff; the set design was by Narelle Sissons; the lighting design was by James Vermeulen; the sound design was by Eric DeArmon; the costume design was by Mimi O'Donnell; the stage manager was Jacki O'Brien; and the production stage manager was Monica Moore. The cast was as follows:

MARCIA	Elizabeth Canavan
NORCA	Liza Colón-Zayas
SONIA	Melissa Feldman
FATHER LUX	Mark Hammer
GAIL	Scott Hudson
ROOFTOP	Ron Cephas Jones
FLIP	Russell G. Jones
VICTOR	Richard Petrocelli
INEZ	Portia
PINKY	Al Roffe
BALTHAZAR	Felix Solis
EDWIN	David Zayas

CHARACTERS

MARCIA

NORCA

SONIA

FATHER LUX

GAIL

ROOFTOP

FLIP

VICTOR

INEZ

PINKY

BALTHAZAR

EDWIN

PLACE

New York City.

TIME

The present.

OUR LADY OF 121ST STREET

ACT ONE

Scene 1

Late morning. Ortiz Funeral Home. Main viewing room. Balthazar and Vic stand in front of an empty casket.

VIC. What kinda fuckin' world is this?!

BALTHAZAR. Mmm.

VIC. I mean, am I alone here?!

BALTHAZAR. "Alone," "not alone" —

VIC. What did she ever do anyway, huh?! What did Rose ever do till the day she died but be a fuckin' living saint on this earth to deserve this, this sacrilege!

BALTHAZAR. Sister Rose was a good woman —

VIC. — There are limits — I don't give a shit! Maybe you grew up in a godless jungle, but I remember when the world was not this! And this? This is not the world!

BALTHAZAR. OK.

VIC. Her fuckin' father, he should rot in hell! That's first off! Demons should shit in his mouth daily, the Irish punk! Don't take much guts to beat on a woman, ya get me?

BALTHAZAR. I wasn't aware of her history —

VIC. — Why you think she became a nun anyway, beautiful girl like that? All this "needle exchange," "alcoholic drunk tank" she had runnin' up here? "Gangs" this, "stop the violence" that? All that thankless shit she did? Was it because she was a good person? Sure. But if ya look underneath it all, it's two things: She donned

7

the habit because she was terrified of intimacy, and all them programs was a way to atone for the sins of her fuckin' piece-of-dirt Shanty-Irish Mick-fuck father!

BALTHAZAR. — Hey, what's your name?

VIC. My name?

BALTHAZAR. Yeah, friend, tell me your name.

VIC. It's Victor. Why?

BALTHAZAR. You wanna drink, Vic? A little nip? Take the edge off?

VIC. I prefer to keep my edge on, pal. *(Balthazar drinks from a half-pint bottle.)*

BALTHAZAR. Gotta ask you about your pants, Vic.

VIC. My pants?

BALTHAZAR. You are aware that you're not wearing pants?

VIC. Of course I'm aware — they stole 'em!

BALTHAZAR. Where'd you sleep last night, Vic?

VIC. I slept here last night, and my name is Victor, not Vic.

BALTHAZAR. That's quite uncommon, isn't it? A mourner sleeping over at a wake? —

VIC. What are you, a cop?

BALTHAZAR. No, Vic, I'm a farmer. I came here to sell some eggs.

VIC. You accusing me of something?!

BALTHAZAR. I'm sorry. I'm not accusing, sir, just, I get a call, I come here, there's a man ranting in his underwear, a missing corpse, no sign of forced entry — and it's not the corpse of Ned the Wino or Bobo the Clown that's been stolen, it's our Sister Rose, sir. Sister Rose.

VIC. Look, I came over in the mornin' yesterday, it was a fuckin' madhouse in here, OK?! Crackhead junkies, politicians, reporters, screaming babies, I had ta leave. I came back at closin', tossed the funeral guy a coupla hundred bucks ... I wanted, I needed a little time, alright?!

BALTHAZAR. OK.

VIC. I knew her my whole life since we were six for Christ's sake.

BALTHAZAR. I understand.

VIC. These fuckin' people, yesterday? Some of them showin' up in dirty jeans and T-shirts?! Eating pizza?! Little kids with video games makin' loud electrical noises?! I mean, "What goes on here," no?! ... I saw one mothahfuckah kneelin' in front of Rose's casket, he's prayin', then his fuckin' cell phone goes off and he ... he fuckin' answers it! Has a goddamn conversation in Spanish, and not a short one ... Talkin' loud too, "Mira, mira, mira" — kneelin' over

8

her fuckin' casket! I mean, what the fuck is that, mister?! Can you tell me?! 'Cuz I'm at a loss over here —

BALTHAZAR. Grief takes different forms.

VIC. That ain't grief! I don't know what the fuck that is, but it ain't grief!

BALTHAZAR. ... I once knew a guy — hey now, listen ta me.

VIC. I'm here.

BALTHAZAR. True story: ... I once knew a guy, a coupla detectives went to his apartment to inform him that his son had been raped and murdered in the playground up on 137th —

VIC. — Jesus —

BALTHAZAR. You know what his reaction was? And keep in mind this is a man who loved his son dearly, OK? ... His reaction was: He wouldn't leave the house to I.D. the body until after the Knick game was over ... It was "the playoffs," he said ... They watched the whole fourth quarter together in silence ... He served them ham sandwiches with warm beer ... And this was a man who lived ... for his son *(Balthazar takes another swig from his bottle.)* ... I am going to close this casket now. You are going to go outside and speak to my partner. He will secure you a new pair of pants. Where you live, Vic? Brooklyn? Queens?

VIC. Staten Island.

BALTHAZAR. We'll have a squad car drive you home.

VIC. I'm here for the duration.

BALTHAZAR. OK. Crime Scene needs to work through this room now, Vic. When they're done, the room will be open again. OK?

VIC. Fine.

BALTHAZAR. My partner's outside in front of a black and grey Ford. Ya can't miss him, he's Chinese and he walks with a pronounced limp.

VIC. For the record, I had nuthin' to do with this.

BALTHAZAR. I don't think that you did.

VIC. Just make sure you catch the mothahfuckah.

BALTHAZAR. Sister Rose was my teacher. I liked her very much.

VIC. ... Ya know, if Rudy were still in office, this woulda never happened — I'm sure of it! He wouldn't of took this lyin' down for two seconds.

BALTHAZAR. ... My partner — he's right outside.

VIC. Right ... Say ... Did they ever catch that guy?

BALTHAZAR. What guy?

VIC. The guy who murdered the kid.

BALTHAZAR. No ... No, not yet.

VIC. What, uh, what ever happened to the guy with the ham sandwiches?

BALTHAZAR. ... The guy with the ham sandwiches?

VIC. Yeah ...

BALTHAZAR. Why? You want one?

VIC. One what?

BALTHAZAR. A ham sandwich.

VIC. Do I...?

BALTHAZAR. It's a joke, Vic. I'm joking.

VIC. Not funny. Not funny at all.

Scene 2

The church. Walter "Rooftop" Desmond confesses.

ROOFTOP. Bless me Father for I have sinned ... *(Pause.)* ... a lot, know what I'm sayin'? ... Yes sir ... Um ... Are you, Are you there, Father? ...

FATHER LUX. Yes.

ROOFTOP. Alright, juss checkin' ... That you, Father Martin?

FATHER LUX. Uh, no.

ROOFTOP. Father Cunningham?

FATHER LUX. No.

ROOFTOP. Oh ... Where Father Cunningham at?

FATHER LUX. Excuse me?

ROOFTOP. I say, where Father Cunningham at?

FATHER LUX. Father Cunningham?

ROOFTOP. Yeah.

FATHER LUX. He's — no longer with us.

ROOFTOP. Father C, you talkin' 'bout?

FATHER LUX. Yes.

ROOFTOP. "No longer with us," huh?

FATHER LUX. Yes.

ROOFTOP. Father C?

FATHER LUX. Correct.

ROOFTOP. Dag ... He didn't do something "bad," did he?

FATHER LUX. He's dead.

ROOFTOP. Dead?!

FATHER LUX. With God, yes.

ROOFTOP. Well, pardon me, but — why didn't you just say that then?

FATHER LUX. What?

ROOFTOP. I'm sayin', if the man's dead, juss say he dead.

FATHER LUX. I did.

ROOFTOP. Nah, you said "no longer with us" — like, like a "scandal" or something.

FATHER LUX. Are you here to make confession, sir?

ROOFTOP. Yes I am, but Father C was a close, personal friend of mine, and I can't really say I appreciate —

FATHER LUX. Father Cunningham has been dead for fifteen years, sir, OK?! *(Pause.)*

ROOFTOP. Oh … OK … Sorry …

FATHER LUX. … So, how long since your last confession?

ROOFTOP. My last confession?

FATHER LUX. Yes.

ROOFTOP. The last one?

FATHER LUX. Yes.

ROOFTOP. You mean in a church?

FATHER LUX. In a church. Yes.

ROOFTOP. Right. Well … last one been … well … well, it's been … Know what I'm sayin? It's been been. Definitely been been.

FATHER LUX. OK.

ROOFTOP. Put it like this: my first confession? That was the last time checkin' in with y'all, so, yeah, been a while … been … well —

FATHER LUX. Got it. Proceed.

ROOFTOP. 'Cuz I mean, ya know, my moms raised me right, went to school right upstairs, listened ta the nuns, Sister Rose and all, still … Shit! Is Father C really dead?!

FATHER LUX. What?

ROOFTOP. 'Cuz I was hopin' ta get Father C.

FATHER LUX. Sir —

ROOFTOP. Guess everybody got ta go, right?

FATHER LUX. Yes.

ROOFTOP. Still, how's a man gonna up and die with no warning?

FATHER LUX. Sir —

ROOFTOP. Send a telegram, sumpthin': "Might die soon. FYI."

FATHER LUX. Perhaps you ought to collect yourself and come

11

back later.

ROOFTOP. Hey Father, did you know that Father C one time got hit by a Mack truck but he was OK?

FATHER LUX. Sir —

ROOFTOP. See, us kids, we was playin' Booties Up on the wall across from here, but we was all standin' in the street like fools do, and —

FATHER LUX. Stop.

ROOFTOP. What, I can't relate a little anecdote?

FATHER LUX. What you can do, sir, is confess.

ROOFTOP. Confess, huh?

FATHER LUX. Confess your sins. Yes.

ROOFTOP. Dag, you all business, aint'cha, Father?

FATHER LUX. Sir —

ROOFTOP. No prelude nuthin' — just spit it out.

FATHER LUX. — Sir —

ROOFTOP. — "Early birds eat apples and worms," I gotcha — got no argument wit' that.

FATHER LUX. OK then.

ROOFTOP. You got a forthright nature, Father — no nonsense — I respect that in a man.

FATHER LUX. Oh. Well —

ROOFTOP. Still, even Hank Aaron hit a few off the practice tee before he stepped up to the rock — gotta marinate before ya grill, right?

FATHER LUX. This is not a "cook-out," sir.

ROOFTOP. No, it's not —

FATHER LUX. No charcoal, no anecdotes, no franks and beans —

ROOFTOP. — True 'dat —

FATHER LUX. This is, in fact, a confessional, sir. A confessional — not a "conversational" — do you understand that distinction?

ROOFTOP. I'll keep it moving.

FATHER LUX. Thank you.

ROOFTOP. OK ... right: So ... So, yeah — I mean, whaddyacallit? The inter Venal Sins?

FATHER LUX. Venal.

ROOFTOP. What?

FATHER LUX. Venal.

ROOFTOP. Venal yeah — mucho venal. Venal Sins, dass daily, daily occurrence. Prolly racked up a dozen since I walked up in here ... And, uh, Mortal Sins? Mortal Sins, Father? I mean, "pick

12

a Commandment, any Commandment," know what I'm sayin'?
FATHER LUX. How 'bout you pick one?
ROOFTOP. Oh ... OK ... uh ... Dag, Father, I'm juss, I'm juss a
bad man, Father. Lyin', cheatin', stealin', and humpin' — Dag.
Freebasing ... See, I'm the kind a guy ... one time I ... well, there
was this girl once ... say Father, I can't smoke in here, right?

Scene 3

Flip and Gail by the bathroom — midstream.

FLIP. — Do not act like a faggot!
GAIL. Excuse you?
FLIP. Put your collar down!
GAIL. My collar?
FLIP. Where'd that scarf come from?! You were not wearing that
scarf when we left the hotel, Gail!
GAIL. You said we were coming here as a couple Robert!
FLIP. And I changed my mind! And you know that I changed my
mind because I been tellin' you all fuckin' morning, Gail, that I
changed my fuckin' mind — so just lose the scarf, do not act like
a faggot, and stop calling me fuckin' "Robert"!
GAIL. What should I call you? Penelope?
FLIP. Flip, goddamnit! For the fifty-eighth time, they call me Flip!
GAIL. Flip what? Flip a pancake? Flip a flappy Flip Flop?
FLIP. Gail —
GAIL. Maybe I should have a special name too, like ... "Rocky."
FLIP. Stop it —
GAIL. — I could be "Hercules," grow a beard.
FLIP. Look! You're an "actor," right? So juss act like you're not a fag-
got for a few fuckin' hours if that's not fuckin' beneath you, OK?!
GAIL. Cursing.
FLIP. I will not have this today, Gail! Do you hear me? Will not
have it!
GAIL. Will not have what, Robert? A relationship? A partner? The
respect of the man who lays beside you at night?
FLIP. You know who I am, and you know how I feel about you!

13

GAIL. ... Do I?

FLIP. Don't do this today, Gail.

GAIL. My friends embraced you, Robert! My parents took you in!

FLIP. Your friends are all gay, Gail, and your parents trumpet my race and sexuality with glee 'cuz it makes them feel like better liberals!

GAIL. I'm going to tell them you said that!

FLIP. Good. Why don't you hop on the next plane and tell them in person.

GAIL. Do you really mean that? Do you?

FLIP. You know what? I ain't even tryin' ta have this conversation!

GAIL. "Ain't even tryin'"?!

FLIP. Dass what I said!

GAIL. Right, "assimilation." Going back ta the "Hood," can't be you, gotta be someone you never were.

FLIP. Careful now —

GAIL. No, Robert, you're the one who should be careful! — didn't you ever see *The Death of Sunny* with Shelley Winters?

FLIP. Gail —

GAIL. Sunny Waldman denied her Jewishness before a Nazi tribunal to avoid the death camps — and what happened to Sunny? She became a morphine-addicted harlot who ended up wandering into the forests of Bavaria to be consumed by wolves and jackals — that's what! Denial's like a pair of Prada silk pajamas, Robert — the price is just too high!

FLIP. Look, Drama Empress: Just turn it down a few notches and be here for me. Quiet and dignified. Can you do that, yes or no?!

GAIL. "Turn it down a few notches"?

FLIP. Yes or no, Gail!

GAIL. I am not a Drama Emperess!

FLIP. I am begging you, OK? Begging.

GAIL. On my worst day, I'm more masculine than you.

FLIP. Gail —

GAIL. I'm like a young Al Pacino: intense, soulful —

FLIP. Oh, you aren't a "young" anything, Gail! And you certainly, certainly ain't no Al Pacino! *(Inez exits bathroom.)*

INEZ. Flip Johnson, shit! — is that really you?!

FLIP. Inez Smith?! Dag girl, you're lookin' too fine! Oh Jesus — How long it's been?

INEZ. Nevah mind all that. You look so good, Flip! How come you look so good?

FLIP. 'Cuz I'm lookin' at you, Inez Smith!

14

INEZ. Aw Flip! Flip! ... Who's this man, Flip?

FLIP. Ah, Inez, I'd like you to meet my colleague, this is —

GAIL. Goliath. Goliath Muscleton.

INEZ. Goliath, huh?

FLIP. Goliath is one of my partners at the firm.

INEZ. Oh, well that's nice.

FLIP. Yeah it is.

INEZ. I guess things must be pretty progressive out there in Wisconsin. Maybe I should move there.

GAIL. What do you mean?

INEZ. I mean, a black man and a gay man, partners in the same firm —

FLIP. I'm not gay Inez.

INEZ. I'm not talkin' 'bout you honey, I'm talkin' 'bout Goliath here — *(To Gail.)* Now you stay away from my man now, girl —

FLIP. — Say. How's Rooftop doin'?

INEZ. Oh, Me and Walter divorced fifteen years now, baby, I hope the bastard's got leukemia.

GAIL. *(To Inez.)* So I look gay to you, but "Flip" doesn't? I wonder why that is?

FLIP. Maybe 'cuz you homosexual, and I'm not. *(To Inez.)* Now how's that for a theory?

INEZ. Sounds good to me. Anyway, I'm gettin' ready to move on, Flip. I gotta go meet Norca before the wake.

FLIP. Nasty Norca? How is she?

INEZ. Fucked up and forgotten, so I'm told ... Haven't seen her in years.

FLIP. Now why's that?

INEZ. 'Cuz she slept wit' Walter, fuckin' ho.

FLIP. Say what?!

INEZ. Please. Walter cherry-popped every Jordache bubble-butt from 96th on up, served me right to be so damn naive ... Comin' home with tar stains all on his sweatpants. Pigeon feathers. And ta think, I thought y'all called him "Rooftop" 'cuz he was tall ... We gonna have a drink tonight, baby?

FLIP. Shit, "do a cow got lips"?

INEZ. Do a cow got what?! "Lips," Flip?!

FLIP. It's, it's an expression ...

INEZ. "Do a cow got lips"?! — Oh, Flip Johnson! Flip Johnson, you are just so cute I could eat your little fine-ass self alive —

FLIP. — You know how we do —

INEZ. — You done gone country up there in Wisconsin, ain't cha?!

GAIL. Yee-haw.

INEZ. ... "Do a cow got lips"? — I'm a haveta try that one out on my peoples in Bed-Stuy! —

FLIP. — Anyway — tonight baby, after: It's you, me, and a pitcher a margaritas — and I'll be lookin' forward to that.

INEZ. Alright then ... Flip, do I look old?

FLIP. Girl, you're the Fountain of Youth.

INEZ. Thank you. Well, nice to meet you, Ulysses.

GAIL. Goliath.

INEZ. Shame about Sister Rose, huh? I heard they found her on the curb.

FLIP. Heart attack?

INEZ. Alcohol.

FLIP. What?

INEZ. Yeah — now they can't find her at all.

FLIP. How you mean?

INEZ. They stole her body and the pants off a white man.

FLIP. What?

INEZ. They gonna bury an empty box in the mornin' if she don't turn up. Well ... Bye baby *(Inez exits. Pause.)*

GAIL. What were you inferring when you said that I "certainly, certainly, was no Al Pacino"?

FLIP. What?!

GAIL. I want to know what you meant by that.

FLIP. Gail?!

GAIL. Because if you're inferring that I'm not a good actor —

FLIP. Gail, I just got some unsettling news.

GAIL. So did I. According to you, I can't act!

FLIP. Why are you talking about this?!

GAIL. And you didn't just say "certainly," you said "certainly, certainly," like, "Oh, certainly, certainly" —

FLIP. — Go back to the hotel, Gail!

GAIL. I don't want to be with somebody who doesn't respect what I do!

FLIP. Oh yeah?! Well, you're a fuckin' lousy actor, Gail — not "not good," lousy! You're the worst actor in the state of Wisconsin — and that's no easy feat!

GAIL. That's not true.

FLIP. Oh, it is true! When's the last time you made a fuckin' dime acting anyway? Never! That's when.

GAIL. I studied with Lee Strasberg!

FLIP. That's prolly what killed him! *(Flip drinks from the flask.)*

GAIL. ... You're upset, you're angry with me, that's why you're being cruel right now, saying things that you know aren't true.

FLIP. I know when I go to a theatre and something sucks ass, Gail! —

GAIL. If you're referring to my Torvald —

FLIP. I'm referring to your everything! You did that show with the kids and fuckin' five-year olds were acting circles 'round you! Everything you're in, you're the worst fucking one! Ask our friends! Ask anyone who knows you! You suck, OK?! You accuse me of denial?! Look at your own self, Gail!

GAIL. ... At least ...

FLIP. At least what? I know who I am — I'm a lawyer, Gail! And what are you — other than a fuckin' self-centered, drunk, swishing community theatre housewife!

GAIL. ... I am not that fem.

FLIP. Whatever!

GAIL. So you admit I'm not that fem? *(Flip drinks.)*

FLIP. ... I am so tolerant of your weaknesses, Gail. I really am. But you? You have no empathy for anything that goes against what you want when you want it.

GAIL. Robert —

FLIP. You think joint checking was easy for me?! I have your name on everything that's mine, and I've put in the work every day for the last two years to allow myself to keep growing closer to you.

GAIL. And I applaud that —

FLIP. Inez ain't stupid, Gail. All I asked for was the respect to handle my business, in my neighborhood, with my people, at my own pace and in my own way. You couldn't even give me that.

GAIL. Where you goin'?

FLIP. I don't know.

GAIL. Can I come?

FLIP. Get away.

GAIL. ... So are we still together?

Scene 4

Norca and Balthazar.

BALTHAZAR. Last night, Norca, between ten P.M. and nine A.M., where were you?

NORCA. I was at your mother's house fuckin' her in her ass wit' a strap on — dass where I was!

BALTHAZAR. Very funny.

NORCA. You see anybody laughin'? I know your mothah ain't laughin' — I drove that bitch's head through the wall, her hair all covered in plaster an' shit ... I could go now, "Ossifer"?!

BALTHAZAR. Detective.

NORCA. Rent-a-cop! Fisher Price Bitch! *(Balthazar takes a drink from his flask.)*

BALTHAZAR. Where are your kids these days, Norca? Spofford? Foster care? Rikers?

NORCA. Where's your kid, Balthazar? Oh, yeah — he in a cemetery, all raped up and dead, ain't that right, Mr. Parent?! Mr. Judgmental alcoholic mothahfuckah! *(Balthazar smiles.)*

BALTHAZAR. I hope you took her, Norca.

NORCA. Took who?

BALTHAZAR. "Took who"?

NORCA. I ain't stuttered. Took who, mothahfuckah?!

BALTHAZAR. You're very smart, Norca. You always been smart. That brain of yours, it hurts to carry it around, doesn't it?

NORCA. It's been five seconds, Balthazar, don't you need another drink?

BALTHAZAR. The next time I take you into custody, Norca, I won't slap you on the wrist — no — the next time, Norca, I'm gonna send your ass to Bellevue —

NORCA. — Fuck you —

BALTHAZAR. — And when you get to Bellevue, you gonna bug out, Norca! You gonna hit somebody, or wild out somehow, and they gonna start medicating your ass. Then, you gonna be real fucked up, and they gonna send you to Creedmore for mental rehabilitation! You know you can't sign yourself out of Creedmore, right?

18

NORCA. Why you fuckin' with me?

BALTHAZAR. You must of visited Creedmore, right? Half your family passed through there, no? ... That brain of yours, Norca? That brain you love so much even though it's killin' you? Creedmore gonna snatch that brain, Norca. Snatchy, snatchy, no more brain! No more Norca. They gonna snatch your brain, and before you know it, you gonna weigh 300 pounds, have hair where God didn't intend, and you gonna have one of those faces — you know those faces I'm talking about, right Norca? The institutionalized face? The "no more brain, smile like a three-year-old" face? The "I've been downgraded from a human to a mammal" face. No more Nasty Norca, you're gonna be a mammal!

NORCA. I ain't no mammal!

BALTHAZAR. Then tell me where she is!

NORCA. Where who is?!

BALTHAZAR. Where is she?

NORCA. Where is motherfuckin' who?!

BALTHAZAR. Where is she?

NORCA. I don't know what you talkin' 'bout!

BALTHAZAR. You're lyin.

NORCA. No I ain't!

BALTHAZAR. You're a fuckin' liar.

NORCA. Don't be breathin' up on me!

BALTHAZAR. Liar.

NORCA. Liar, what?!

BALTHAZAR. Where is she?

NORCA. Where is who?!

BALTHAZAR. Where is she?

NORCA. You want me to bust you in your mothahfuckin' face?!

BALTHAZAR. Yes. I would like very much for you to bust me in my mothahfuckin' face, Mammal Girl. Please hit me. Please.

NORCA. I'll do it, ya drunk-ass bitch!

BALTHAZAR. Please.

NORCA. I will!

BALTHAZAR. Hit me. Right now, Norca. Hit me now!

Scene 5

Funeral home waiting room: Edwin and Pinky.

EDWIN. *(To himself.)* "Sister Rose Marie was a very special person. I, personally, had her for homeroom for first grade, and for second grade, and then for second grade again, and then for second grade one more time, which is why I respected (No, not respected), which is why, even though she beat my ass wit' a shilaylee. (Nah, dat ain't right.)

PINKY. Edwin —

EDWIN. "We always loved her, even when we didn't" —

PINKY. Edwin —

EDWIN. Shut up, Pinky, I'm tryin' ta put my thoughts in place —

PINKY. Oh ... OK.

EDWIN. Put that cigarette out, you can't smoke in here.

PINKY. Sorry —

EDWIN. Wait. Gimme a drag first ... "We loved her 'cuz" —

PINKY. You want a fresh one?

EDWIN. Nah ... Yeah. Whatchu smokin'?

PINKY. Kool Breeze.

EDWIN. Kool Breeze? What the fuck kinda brand is dat?

PINKY. Two dollar-eighty-five.

EDWIN. Fuck dat ... You got any chocolate?

PINKY. I could get some.

EDWIN. You could get me two packs a Yodels?

PINKY. You wanna juss split a box?

EDWIN. Nah ... Yeah. You need money?

PINKY. Maybe juss like four dollars.

EDWIN. In other words, you need money.

PINKY. I guess.

EDWIN. So juss say dat then.

PINKY. I didn't wanna upset your concentration.

EDWIN. Well, it's upset.

PINKY. Sorry.

EDWIN. Not on account a you, Pink, alright?

PINKY. ... OK.

EDWIN. Are you sayin' "OK" like you believe me? Or, are you juss sayin', "OK"?

PINKY. Like I believe you.

EDWIN. Are you sure? I don' wanna see you start cryin', 'cuz, I juss couldn't handle that right now.

PINKY. I ain't gonna cry.

EDWIN. I mean, if you feel like cryin', cry. 'Cuz I don' wanna stifle your feelins or nuthin' —

PINKY. I ain't stifled.

EDWIN. It's juss, I need you strong over here.

PINKY. I'm strong ... Wanna feel my muscle?

EDWIN. Look, here's a twenty-dollar bill, OK? Wit' the Yodels? Get a quart a milk.

PINKY. OK.

EDWIN. Regular, not skim or some shit. The red one.

PINKY. I know.

EDWIN. And check the date. On the Yodels too. Grab the milk from the back.

PINKY. I got three girlfriends, Edwin.

EDWIN. That's great. Bring me the change.

PINKY. They're all pretty ... except one.

EDWIN. I gotta get back to this, Pinky.

PINKY. OK ... You're gonna make a great Analogy, Edwin.

EDWIN. Eulogy, Pinky. Not analogy. Eulogy.

PINKY. I'm gonna tell her all about it when I get home.

EDWIN. Great ... Tell who?

PINKY. Sister Rose.

EDWIN. Pinky ... Bro ... Sister Rose is dead, you know dat right?

PINKY. I know.

EDWIN. Dead, like, dead.

PINKY. I know.

EDWIN. Like Mom and Dad, right?

PINKY. Yeah ... And the Super. Mr. Regal.

EDWIN. Yeah ... Dead like them, right?

PINKY. In Heaven.

EDWIN. Dass right ...

PINKY. Eatin' cheeseburgers.

EDWIN. Watchin' Pay-Per-View for free with the Blessed Mother and Saint Anthony, and Mom and Dad.

PINKY. And Mr. Regal.

EDWIN. Yes ... Now, Pinky: When Balthazar's partner came in

here and asked us those questions, you answered the truth, right?

PINKY. Whaddya mean?

EDWIN. I mean, if I were to go up to our apartment right now, I wouldn't find anyone that ain't supposed to be there, right?

PINKY. ... You mean like Mrs. McNulty's cat?

EDWIN. Never mind. Go get the Yodels now.

PINKY. I wantcha to meet my girlfriends.

EDWIN. I'm lookin' forward to it ... Yodels. Go. *(Pause.)*

PINKY. I didn't mean to upset your concentration, Edwin.

EDWIN. I know that Pinky.

PINKY. I think ... can I say something, Edwin?

EDWIN. Is it sumpthin' short?

PINKY. Pretty short.

EDWIN. So say it then.

PINKY. Actually, it's two things.

EDWIN. I didn't agree to hearing two things, Pinky.

PINKY. I'll make it quick.

EDWIN. Juss fuckin' say it already.

PINKY. OK: Do you think that girl Norca is gonna be here today and can I have a hug please?

EDWIN. How many hugs have I given you today?

PINKY. Only like six.

EDWIN. So go get the Yodels and milk, bring me the change, and I'll give you another hug. How's that?

PINKY. A long hug?

EDWIN. Would you just get the fuckin' Yodels already?!

PINKY. Oh. OK ... What about Norca?

EDWIN. Forget about Norca, she don't like you. Eat some Yodels and forget about that shit.

PINKY. I really would feel better if you —

EDWIN. Oh fuckin' Jesus fuckin' Christ Pinky! Come over here! *(Pinky crosses to Edwin. They hug. Marcia enters.)*

MARCIA. Oh, excuse me.

PINKY. Hello lady.

MARCIA. Hi ... *(Smells.)* Was someone smoking in here?

PINKY. You wanna be my girlfriend?

MARCIA. Uh, I don't know. Maybe? ...

PINKY. I'm going to get some Yodels for me and my brother Edwin.

MARCIA. Oh.

PINKY. You look like Sister Rose.

22

MARCIA. She was my aunt.

PINKY. I'm getting Yodels now.

MARCIA. Well, nice to meet you.

PINKY. Can I touch your butt?

EDWIN. Pinky! Go get the Yodels.

PINKY. OK. Bye, lady. *(Pinky exits.)*

EDWIN. Hello, sorry for that. I'm, uh, Edwin Velasquez.

MARCIA. Marcia Cook, could you open up that window, please?!

EDWIN. It's closed 'cuz of the A.C.

MARCIA. So smoke outside! I'm sorry but I'm an asthmatic!

EDWIN. Ass-what?

MARCIA. Asthma? Hello! I have asthma. I mean the sign says, "Prohibido Fumar," right? But, of course, I'm the bitch, just because other people don't give a hoot about anyone else except themselves, so they have no goddamned —

EDWIN. Hey look —

MARCIA. I mean, I could die! OK?! I could literally have an asthma attack and drop dead right here! So I'd appreciate it if you would stop gawking at me and open the damn window before I start to really get upset!

EDWIN. It's open, it's open!

MARCIA. I'm really sorry —

EDWIN. Apology accepted.

MARCIA. Apology? ... See, that's the whole problem right there. I shouldn't have to go off on people and get labeled some kind of overreacting person just to get them to obey a damn law which they're supposed to just obey because it's the goddamn' law! I shouldn't have to even ask!

EDWIN. You're very right —

MARCIA. I mean, I didn't put up that "No Smoking" sign —

EDWIN. No, you didn't —

MARCIA. Cuz if there was a sign here that said, "Smoking: Mucho Gusto!" I would've just not said a word and suffered silently and possibly died; or I would've just found another place to sit, like outside in the stifling humidity or something, OK, because — Don't look at me like that!

EDWIN. Like what?

MARCIA. Like I'm some kind of lunatic, or bitch, or rabble-rouser!

EDWIN. What's a rabble-rouser? *(Marcia collapses.)*

MARCIA. Oh my God!

23

EDWIN. What's wrong?

MARCIA. Palpitations!

EDWIN. Palpi-who?

MARCIA. — Danger! — Danger!

EDWIN. What should I do?

MARCIA. My — inhaler ... please ... my — bag.

EDWIN. What? This?

MARCIA. Oh God — Yes — Thank *(Marcia inhales deeply several times.)*

EDWIN. Should I call 911?

MARCIA. No! Oh God! Danger! — I'm — "count ten, Marcia" — ten, nine, five.

EDWIN. Eight.

MARCIA. ... Eight?

EDWIN. *(Helping her.)* ... Seven ...

MARCIA. ... Six?

EDWIN. Dass right —

MARCIA and EDWIN. ... Five ... four ... three ... two ... one. *(Pause.)*

MARCIA. Oh my God.

EDWIN. That was scary.

MARCIA. Oh my God.

EDWIN. It's OK.

MARCIA. Hold me?

EDWIN. Yeah ... Yeah, sure. *(Edwin cradles Marcia. A beat.)*

MARCIA. ... You saved my life.

EDWIN. Actually I was one of the smokers that caused your conniption.

MARCIA. — Look, I rarely feel grateful for anything, so could you just shut up and let me be grateful for a second? *(Pause.)*

EDWIN. You're a very strange lady.

MARCIA. Ssh. *(Pause.)*

EDWIN. ... Are you sad about Sister Rose's body gettin' vicked?

MARCIA. No.

EDWIN. ... Do you think —

MARCIA. Pipe down! People get so intimidated by silence, they just wanna talk, talk, talk — *(Pause.)* Are you touching my breast?

EDWIN. That was accidental.

MARCIA. Oh.

EDWIN. ... You were very nice to my brother.

MARCIA. Well, I was raised to be kind to the disabled — I mean —

EDWIN. That's OK ...

MARCIA. I didn't mean to infer —

EDWIN. He ain't retarded, he just suffered a accident when we was little. I accidently threw a brick out the window which ended up on his head.

MARCIA. ... I'm sorry.

EDWIN. ... Are you, are you crying?

MARCIA. I just, any time I see someone like that, you know, it just makes me very sad, like I should be nicer to people ... or devote more time to charities ... Something ... Something. You know?

EDWIN. So why don't you just do that then?

MARCIA. ... What?

EDWIN. I said, Do it then. Help out more.

MARCIA. Look, I help out plenty already —

EDWIN. But maybe you could do more —

MARCIA. OK, like, back off?

EDWIN. Back off?

MARCIA. You know nothing about me, or what I do or don't do! When's the last time you wrote a check or helped an old lady cross the street?

EDWIN. Um ... I'm not sure.

MARCIA. Right. So ... "People in glass houses," OK, mister?!

EDWIN. People in glass houses what?

MARCIA. You know!

EDWIN. I know what?

MARCIA. You've never heard that before?!

EDWIN. Why would anyone wanna live in a glass house? It could break, or, people could peep at you —

MARCIA. You know what? I've gotta find my friend Sonia.

EDWIN. Did I say something wrong?

MARCIA. Look: Goodbye, thanks for saving me.

EDWIN. Why donchu hang out, have a Yodel?

MARCIA. I'm allergic to chocolate.

EDWIN. Have a soda then.

MARCIA. Caffeine?

EDWIN. How 'bout a slice a pizza?

MARCIA. Pizza! Hello? Cheese?! God, did someone throw a brick on your head too?! *(Marcia exits.)*

Scene 6

Inez and Norca. Bar and grill.

INEZ. So I tol' that nigger; "If the shit can't stay up, then put the damn thing away," OK?
NORCA. You said that shit?!
INEZ. Sister, please. Then he say, "Maybe if you" — and he start makin' this gesture, like he afraid ta say, "Put yo mouth on me," so instead he juss tries ta mime it, like.
NORCA. No he didn't!
INEZ. Oh yes he did!
NORCA. No class fool —
INEZ. So I tol' the driver ta pull over, and I kicked his ass out the damn cab.
NORCA. Cab?!
INEZ. Ended up I fucked the cabby.
NORCA. You was in a cab?!
INEZ. Shit, I was fifteen, girl, know what I'm sayin'?
NORCA. You nevah fucked no nigga in a cab!
INEZ. Yes I did! Fine Haitian man — He was sending money home to his mom to buy, like, a new hut or something.
NORCA. "A hut"?
INEZ. Sumpthin' like that — house, hut — you know them Haitians back then —
NORCA. Girl, you crazy.
INEZ. Anyway, you wasn't around. You was — I think you was wit' that Eustace Mejias at the time.
NORCA. Oh ma Gawd! Little Eustace.
INEZ. That ain't what I heard.
NORCA. Heard?! Girl, stop lyin'.
INEZ. Awright, I had me some Eustace, but that was long after you were finished wit' him.
NORCA. ... Yeah, well ... you know ...
INEZ. I think you was datin' that bank robber by then.
NORCA. He wasn't no robber. He was a suspect!
INEZ. Well, I never met the suspect.

NORCA. ... Dag Inez, you funny.

INEZ. How you mean?

NORCA. I mean you funny — like how you make your face look when you say shit, like when you said "suspect."

INEZ. My face is my face.

NORCA. See, you doin' it right now!

INEZ. I'm not doin' nuthin'.

NORCA. Yes you are, and it's funny. Dass all. It's a compliment, OK? 'Cuz sometimes I think about funny things you usta say that was funny, or how your face looked like when you was reactin' ta something — like in school — or when we had them sleepovers at your aunt's house — or, like, ya know, all the times we was together — and, I think ta myself, "damn, that bitch was funny," and I wanna juss laugh, and I do laugh, and it's helpful to laugh sometimes — and dass 'cuz of you, so — dass all.

INEZ. Yeah, OK.

NORCA. I ain't tryin' ta say nuthin'.

INEZ. OK, then.

NORCA. ... What? ... You ain't got no compliment for me?

INEZ. ... Well, Norca, other than, "Gee, girl, your fat ass bounced off my kitchen table real nice when you was servin' up your stank pussy to my husband" — other than that, I admit I'm drawing a complete blank.

NORCA. ... Whatever ...

INEZ. That all you got to say?

NORCA. I'm juss tryin' ta have a nice conversation.

INEZ. You fucked my husband!

NORCA. You ain't never missed me after all these years?

INEZ. You fucked my husband!

NORCA. I mean, besides that.

INEZ. Norca — you fucked my husband!

NORCA. How many times I gotta apologize for that?!

INEZ. How about once?!

NORCA. Awright, shit. I apologize, OK?

INEZ. OK.

NORCA. OK, then.

INEZ. OK.

NORCA. I'm juss tryin' ta have a nice conversation.

INEZ. OK ... *(To Sonia.)* Excuse me, Miss, we ain't ruinin' your meal or nuthin', are we?

SONIA. Oh ... No ... I'm just ... Is that ketchup?

27

NORCA. Does it look like ketchup?

INEZ. *(To Norca.)* Girl, stop it. *(To Sonia.)* Here ya go.

SONIA. I'm sorry, I, I'm from Connecticut.

INEZ. Oh yeah? You know New Haven?

SONIA. Um ... yeah?

INEZ. I got some folks up there. Cousins, nephews, all kinds of relations running 'round up there. Good pizza up there in Connecticut. You know about that, Norca?

NORCA. Stop playin'.

INEZ. I'm not playin'. *(To Sonia.)* Tell her.

SONIA. Um.

INEZ. Tell this bitch y'all got the best pizza up there.

SONIA. It's really very good.

NORCA. Not better than New York.

INEZ. *(To Norca.)* You need to get your ass on the Greyhound, try the shit. I'm tellin' you, remember how pizza usta be?

NORCA. Yeah?

INEZ. Well that's how it still is up there. *(To Sonia.)* Am I lyin'?

SONIA. Not as far as I can tell.

NORCA. *(To Inez.)* What she know about how pizza usta be over here?

SONIA. Uh, I've had pizza in New York before. Lots of times. We usta come into the city a lot, you know, for the theatre or a ball game or like my dad usta take us to the Car Show at the Coliseum on 59th —

INEZ. You here for the wake?

SONIA. Yeah.

NORCA. You was a student here?

SONIA. — uh —

NORCA. Hold up, you that bitch, ain't you?! You fuckin' Wendy Elmer, right?!

SONIA. No.

NORCA. I fuckin' hate your ass!

SONIA. I'm not her.

NORCA. Don't lie, bitch! I always thought you was a stuck-up asshole, I fuckin' hate you! Get out my face — fuckin' Wendy Elmer bitch!

INEZ. *(To Inez.)* That ain't Wendy Elmer. Wendy Elmer dead.

NORCA. Dead from what?

INEZ. Dead from the bitch is dead, I don't know from what, I ain't the damn coroner, Wendy Elmer died a long time ago.

28

NORCA. Oh.

INEZ. From a illness I think.

NORCA. Well, good then!

INEZ. Norca, you need ta chill, what the fuck's your problem?

SONIA. She's prolly juss —

NORCA. I could speak for myself, thank you very much!

SONIA. I'm sorry. *(Pause.)*

NORCA. You eat fish, donchu?

SONIA. Eat fish?

NORCA. You a fish eater.

SONIA. I enjoy fish?

NORCA. You suck on females' titties donchu?!

SONIA. You mean am I a lesbian?

INEZ. *(To Norca.)* She ain't no lesbian, Norca. Damn girl, I'm about ta put a muzzle and a leash on you, you are venomous like some kinda no-ear pit-bull. *(To Sonia.)* She's a little tipsy, tipsy and grieving.

NORCA. I ain't grieving! Sister Rose could lick my ass, all I care.

INEZ. Sister Rose was patient with you, Norca.

NORCA. So what she was patient? I ain't tryin' ta say nuthin' bad about the bitch — ain't tryin' ta disrespect her — I'm here, ain't I? I'm representin' for her memory an' shit — I juss don't wanna talk about that penguin bitch! I wanna talk about more funny stories like how you fucked that Haitian motherfucker saving up to buy his moms a hut — light-hearted shit, ya know? Funny! Not fuckin' all this — *(To Sonia.)* Who you think you starin' at?!

SONIA. I'm not starin'.

INEZ. She ain't starin'!

NORCA. *(To Inez.)* Don't tell me the bitch ain't starin'! *(To Sonia.)* You better put yo eyeballs back in your head before someone stomp 'em, ya bug-eyed bitch!

INEZ. *(To Sonia.)* She been drinkin' a little, ya know?

NORCA. *(To Inez.)* Why you takin' her side?!

INEZ. Norca —

NORCA. Doncha "Norca" me; you takin' her side! Why you gotta take her side?! Everywhere I go, someone tryin' ta take the other person's side! Why can't someone take my damn side for once in a while! You juss like my mother, my kids, my P.O., my everybody! Everybody always wanna gang up on me, well, what the fuck did I do, huh?! What the fuck I did so bad that you gotta take the side a some bug-eyed bitch you never met before two minutes ago instead a me who you know practically from fuckin' birth?!

SONIA. I'm gonna go.

INEZ. No. I'm gonna go.

NORCA. No! I'm a go! You ain't gonna abandon me twice! I abandon you! Y'all fuckin' suck, ya know that?! The two of you! Inez, you look older than the hair on my ass, and — You! — I know you Wendy Elmer! You could act like you ain't but — you are fuckin' Wendy Elmer and this is for you from fifth-grade Earth Science — C'mere! *(Norca slaps Sonia across her teeth.)* I never copied off you, anyway!

INEZ. Norca, chill.

NORCA. *(To Sonia.)* If you so smart, why the fuck you live in Connecticut for?!

INEZ. Norca —

NORCA. Connecticut, pizza, eatin', conversation, ruin fuckin' bitch! *(Norca bursts out of the bar in tears.)*

INEZ. Sorry.

SONIA. That's OK, this has happened to me before.

INEZ. It has?

SONIA. Yeah. People always think I'm someone else.

INEZ. ... And then they slap you upside the head?

SONIA. Well, no, but, sometimes, I get the feeling that they want to *(Pause.)*

INEZ. That's ... that's strange.

SONIA. ... Yeah... Yeah, it is.

Scene 7

Rooftop in the confessional.

ROOFTOP. So anyway, Father, 497 sexual interludes. 497 I can think of ... 497, Father ... And that's not including before I was married, and, it's also not including those nights I can't remember due to substances, which, we better just tack on another twenty-five, fifty, 'cuz, I figure it's better to err on the side a caution, doncha think, Father? Yeah. And I mean, the other thing? The "seed spillin"? That's, well, started at eight, average, say, one and a half times a day,

30

I just turned forty, that's thirty-two times 365, uh, zero carry the one, thirteen, carry one, 730, five, nine, ten ... 11,680 plus half a that, say fifty-five hundred give or take, that's over 17,000 solo ventures! — dass alot a seed, Father — alot of "whacky-whacky"! I mean, over 500 counts of adultery, seventeen grand in self-flagellation, "Thou shalt not covet thy neighbor's wife"? I'll be honest, I'm runnin' outta neighbors!

FATHER LUX. ... I smell marijuana.

ROOFTOP. ... Yeah ... Prolly one a them altar boys lighting up, huh?

FATHER LUX. The altar boys are at Bear Mountain today, sir.

ROOFTOP. Bear Mountain?

FATHER LUX. Yes. So —

ROOFTOP. Y'all still doin' that? When I was a altar boy, Father C be takin' us to Bear Mountain every year —

FATHER LUX. Sir —

ROOFTOP. — We'd always be like, "Dag, Father C, Bear Mountain again"?! "Can't we go to like Great Adventure, Jungle Habitat, change it up a little" —

FATHER LUX. — Sir?

ROOFTOP. Yes, Father?

FATHER LUX. The marijuana. I must ask you to extinguish it.

ROOFTOP. Oh ... You wouldn't want a hit before I put it out, would ya, Father?

FATHER LUX. I'd just like you to put it out, sir.

ROOFTOP. Right. Sorry, Padre.

FATHER LUX. It's OK.

ROOFTOP. Nah, I'm a bad man — smokin' weed up in here — temptin' one of God's soldiers wit' some sinsemilla ... You must think I'm some kinda ... Ya think there's any hope for me?

FATHER LUX. Listen, we have weekend retreats for those kind of questions.

ROOFTOP. I'm juss askin' your opinion. Is it not OK to ask?

FATHER LUX. There are people better equipped than me to answer that.

ROOFTOP. Like who?

FATHER LUX. Well, God. Ask God.

ROOFTOP. I'm not ready for God.

FATHER LUX. Or a therapist. Or the Jesuits — they're smart. I'm just, well ... I hear confessions, OK?

ROOFTOP. OK ... But, it's, it's pretty hopeless, right? Right?

31

FATHER LUX. They say despair is the absence of hope. Are you despairing?

ROOFTOP. I am.

FATHER LUX. You know what despair is?

ROOFTOP. The absence of hope, right?

FATHER LUX. Besides that.

ROOFTOP. Oh.

FATHER LUX. Despair is marked by the termination or the cessation of action. For example: A man is stuck in a well —

ROOFTOP. Stuck in a whale?

FATHER LUX. Not a "whale," a well.

ROOFTOP. What's a "well"?

FATHER LUX. A well! You know, you get water from it?

ROOFTOP. Oh, you talkin' about a "well," like, you go wit' your pail to the well? —

FATHER LUX. Yes, a "well."

ROOFTOP. I'm sorry, Father, I thought you said "whale."

FATHER LUX. That's OK, so —

ROOFTOP. 'Cuz there's a story about a man stuck up in a whale, right?

FATHER LUX. That's Jonah.

ROOFTOP. Who?

FATHER LUX. Jo-nah.

ROOFTOP. Yeah, "Jonah," dass right — "Jonah and the Whale"

FATHER LUX. Yes, so —

ROOFTOP. — Sister Rose, she usta tell us that story all the time.

FATHER LUX. It's a nice story —

ROOFTOP. I usta go home and have nightmares 'bout gettin' stuck up inside a whale — my pops usta beat my ass wit' a slipper talkin' 'bout, "Ain't no whales in Harlem, fool, go back ta sleep, this is a workin' family!" ... Yeah ...

FATHER LUX. Anyway —

ROOFTOP. Say, you remember them pajamas wit' the feet on 'em? You ever had a pair?

FATHER LUX. No.

ROOFTOP. Dass too bad, they was snug. An' I always usta like those little glove clips they would put on your coat, with the long string runnin' through your sleeves, so your gloves was always hangin' there when ya needed them? I mean, I can't tell you how many pairs of nice leather gloves I usta lose every winter — I mean, this is before I moved out to Los Angeles —

FATHER LUX. Sir?

ROOFTOP. I once lost a pair of genuine mink-lined Italian leather gloves —

FATHER LUX. Sir?

ROOFTOP. Yes, Father?

FATHER LUX. Confessional! Not "conversational"! Remember?!

ROOFTOP. Right, right.

FATHER LUX. There may be others waiting.

ROOFTOP. Waiting for what?

FATHER LUX. Waiting.

ROOFTOP. Others?

FATHER LUX. Others. Yes.

ROOFTOP. ... You tryin' ta get rid of me, Father?

FATHER LUX. No.

ROOFTOP. You got a little egg timer back there or sumpthin'?

FATHER LUX. No egg timer, no.

ROOFTOP. 'Cuz maybe you didn't hear me when I said I ain't made a confession for thirty years.

FATHER LUX. I heard you.

ROOFTOP. You have any idea how hard it is to walk into a church after thirty years, Father?

FATHER LUX. The important thing is that you came back.

ROOFTOP. Dass right I came back — and it's not like y'all got the most alluring marketing campaign going on these days either, Father. You feelin' me?

FATHER LUX. I feel you.

ROOFTOP. And, ya know, forgive me Father, but it ain't like y'all the only game in town anymore either! They got all kinda new churches, religions, spiritual growth joints where you can do whatever you want, say whatever you want —

FATHER LUX. — But you came here.

ROOFTOP. That's exactly my point! I came here. So I would think, that after thirty years in the wind Father, that if a fallen sheep comes limpin' back into the manger, that the stable master should just turn off the damn meter and let the sheep say what he need to say in the time he need to say it.

FATHER LUX. In other words, you're more important than those others who may be waiting.

ROOFTOP. What?!

FATHER LUX. I said —

ROOFTOP. Oh see? Dass trickery! Trickery, Father!

FATHER LUX. I don't understand —

ROOFTOP. I came here to feel better, and you tryin' ta send me off feelin' worse!

FATHER LUX. That's not my intention.

ROOFTOP. Them other churches? They don't try ta make a man feel guilty for speakin' his truth. They don't cash their checks off a guilt.

FATHER LUX. You're right.

ROOFTOP. Whaddya mean, "I'm right"?

FATHER LUX. And yet, my question remains: Do you think you're more important than those others who may be waiting?

ROOFTOP. Well obviously, you think the answer to that question is "No"!

FATHER LUX. I didn't say that.

ROOFTOP. Well then, what the hell are you saying?! I mean, shit — when the Prodigal Son came home, his pops killed the fattest calf and had a motherfuckin' banquet! And Noah, Father? Noah gathered up all the animals two by two — he didn't say, "Nah, fuck them chiba-smokin' Zebras, they takin' too long —

FATHER LUX. Sir —

ROOFTOP. The real question here ain't, "Do I think I'm more important?" — the actual damn question is, "Do you think I'm important enough"?!

FATHER LUX. Can you provide me a single, compelling reason why I should?

ROOFTOP. How 'bout 'cuz you're a priest and it's your god-damned job?! Shit, what are you — some kinda rookie?!

FATHER LUX. I've been a priest for forty-six years, sir.

ROOFTOP. Well whatchu been doin' the past half century — playin' pinochle?! Can't you tell when a man is coming to you afraid?

FATHER LUX. Afraid of what?

ROOFTOP. Goddamnit, Father, I'm afraid a everything! Is that what ya wanna hear?! Afraid I'm never gonna be the person I thought I'd be, back when I thought I had all the time in the world to get there! I'm afraid to go next door ta pay my respects to ol' Sister Rose 'cuz my goddamn ex-wife Inez, she's prolly right next door over there at the wake! She don't like me! I don't like me! And I'm afraid that the person I'll like least wherever I go will always be me! ... OK, mothahfuckah?! You happy?! *(Beat.)*

FATHER LUX. My name is Father Lux.

ROOFTOP. Yeah, so what? *(Beat.)*

FATHER LUX. I'm sorry. *(Beat.)*
ROOFTOP. … Lux, huh? You mean, like —
FATHER LUX. Like the soap, yes.
ROOFTOP. I was gonna say Lux as in the Latin, meaning Light.
FATHER LUX. That's impressive. Most people say the soap.
ROOFTOP. Well, I'm not most people.
FATHER LUX. No disputing that.
ROOFTOP. I'm twelve years Catholic school educated — I know my Latin. "Rident stolidi de verba latina" — ain't that right, Father?
FATHER LUX. Yes. Yes it is … Listen, why don't you tell me what brought you to confession today.
ROOFTOP. You mean, like, specifically?
FATHER LUX. Specifically, yes.
ROOFTOP. Uh … *(There is a loud insistent knocking on the confessional door.)*
FATHER LUX. *(To Rooftop.)* Hold on a sec, I'll get rid of him … *(To the knocker.)* Please wait your turn, I'm in the middle of a confession.
BALTHAZAR. Father: This is the New York City Police Department. I'm afraid I must ask the gentleman in the confessional to step out, hands up, and vacate the booth.
FATHER LUX. *(To Rooftop.)* This has never happened to me before.
BALTHAZAR. I repeat: Gentleman in confessional, step out — now.
ROOFTOP. I got weed on me, Father, could you help a brother out?
BALTHAZAR. Gentleman in the confessional, I am drawing my weapon" —
ROOFTOP. — Don't shoot! Don't shoot! *(Rooftop exits the confessional.)*
ROOFTOP. … Balthazar?!
BALTHAZAR. Rooftop! What's up my man?!
ROOFTOP. Mothahfuckah, what the fuck you think you doin?! You scared hell outta me!
BALTHAZAR. Come on brother, I'm with Flip at the bar, I'll buy you a beer.
ROOFTOP. A beer?! Balthazar — I'm conductin' some serious business in there with the Father — what I want with a damn beer?
BALTHAZAR. Yo, Rooftop, what's the matter, man? Can't you take a little joke?
ROOFTOP. Joke?! I'm holding a bag of weed and a eight ball of blow on me, brother — cops bangin' down the door on me ain't no joke!

BALTHAZAR. I'm sorry.

ROOFTOP. Jokes like that send mothahfuckahs into intensive care units for fuckin' heart attacks, man!

BALTHAZAR. *(To Rooftop.)* Look, I saw your limo out front. I got excited. I'm sorry. *(To Priest.)* I'm sorry, Father.

ROOFTOP. You OK, Father?

FATHER LUX. I'm fine.

ROOFTOP. ... Where your legs at, Father?

FATHER LUX. Korea. *(Pause.)*

BALTHAZAR. I'll uh, we'll catch up later, right?

ROOFTOP. Hey — someone punch you in yo eye, Balthazar?

BALTHAZAR. Bad day. I'm fine. I'm gonna go. Bye Roof. Father. *(Balthazar crosses to leave.)*

FATHER LUX. *(Re: the confessional.)* Shall we?

ROOFTOP. Yeah, uh — *(To Balthazar.)* Where you say ya going? The bar?

BALTHAZAR. Yeah.

ROOFTOP. The bar at the corner?

BALTHAZAR. Yeah.

ROOFTOP. With Flip Johnson you said?

BALTHAZAR. "Me, Flip, an' a potato chip."

ROOFTOP. Inez ain't down there, is she?

BALTHAZAR. Nah.

ROOFTOP. ... Y'all havin' a little drink, huh?

PRIEST. Uh —

BALTHAZAR. — You wanna come?

ROOFTOP. I mean, a little drink is soothin', ain't no one tryin' ta deny that. *(Pinky enters with grocery bag.)*

PINKY. Rooftop!

ROOFTOP. Oh shit! Wassup, Governor?

BALTHAZAR. Pinky, my man, que pasa?

PINKY. Hi Rooftop.

ROOFTOP. You doin' OK, Governor?

PINKY. Yes.

ROOFTOP. Well alright!

PINKY. I'm going to confession. Then, I'm going to bring these yodels and milk to Edwin so we can eat them.

BALTHAZAR. Man with a plan.

PINKY. Yes. Then, I'm going to find Norca.

ROOFTOP. Well, I won't keep ya then. *(Proffering a bill.)* Say, Guv, you got change for this fiddy?

PINKY. No.

ROOFTOP. *(With a wink.)* Then I guess you gonna haveta hang on to it then.

PINKY. Oh. OK.

ROOFTOP. *(Re: the confessional.)* Go on, handle your business now.

PINKY. Yes.

ROOFTOP. *(Turning to exit.)* Nice rappin' with ya, Padre.

FATHER LUX. *(To Rooftop.)* Sir?

PINKY. I'm ready to confess, Father.

FATHER LUX. *(To Rooftop.)* Sir! Wait! *(To Pinky.)* Ya know what Pinky? Confession is over.

PINKY. But it's not noon, Father.

FATHER LUX. Yeah, but still, it's over.

PINKY. But it's not noon.

FATHER LUX. I know it's not noon.

PINKY. Dass 'cuz it's not noon.

ROOFTOP. Later fellas. *(Rooftop exits.)*

FATHER LUX. Wait!

PINKY. How could it be noon when it's not noon?

FATHER LUX. Sir! —

PINKY. — If it's not noon, Father, then, it's not noon. Cuz if it wasn't noon, but it was noon, then it'd be noon. But, I don't think it's noon, Father. *(Lux turns back to Pinky.)*

FATHER LUX. ... What? *(Beat.)*

PINKY. I brought you some mixed nuts.

FATHER LUX. Oh ... Thanks.

PINKY. Yes. Planters.

FATHER LUX. Great. *(Pinky pecks Lux's cheek.)* Don't do that, Pinky!

PINKY. You looked sad.

FATHER LUX. Don't do that ever.

PINKY. Oh ... Why?

FATHER LUX. Why? ... Just don't do it! *(Beat. Pinky pauses, hoping for a reaction from Lux, doesn't get one. Hands Lux the nuts, exits. Blackout.)*

End of Act One

ACT TWO

Scene 1

Night. Bar and grill, ten P.M.

ROOFTOP. Man, you can't juss sneak me in there for a minute, Balthazar? Flash your badge? Lemme take care of my business? Pay my respects?

BALTHAZAR. Pay your respects to who? There's nothing in there but an empty casket.

ROOFTOP. But there's, like, a photo of her in there, right?

BALTHAZAR. They stole it.

ROOFTOP. Stole the photo? ... Well, how 'bout a mass card then? Sumpthin'. 'Cuz I'm tryin' ta catch the midnight flight out of La Guardia, brother.

BALTHAZAR. You're not staying for the funeral?

ROOFTOP. Nah, man — got my radio joint, six A.M. Prime-time drive time.

BALTHAZAR. I thought we were gonna hang.

ROOFTOP. Balthazar, when we strolled up in this joint, it was day — it ain't day no more. That tells me we been hangin'. Right?

BALTHAZAR. I guess ... Salut.

ROOFTOP. Yeah. Salut, brother. Salut, Flip. *(They drink. Beat.)* So ... I can't, like, go in there for a second, touch the casket, do a little kneel down for a second?

BALTHAZAR. Bro, a crime has been committed. Evidence is being collected. When that's all done, and if Sister Rose's body is found, we'll open up the room.

ROOFTOP. And when's that gonna be?

BALTHAZAR. It's gonna be when it's gonna be. Shit.

ROOFTOP. But the room's gonna open?

BALTHAZAR. What kinda question is that?! How am I supposed to know the answer to that question?!

ROOFTOP. I'm juss inquiring!

38

BALTHAZAR. Look, Rooftop, they're keeping the waiting room open for us all night — so if you wanna go to the waiting room, pay your respects to a lamp and a box of kleenex, and just jet on outta here, then be my fucking guest, OK?

ROOFTOP. You don't have to get all cantankerous, B.

BALTHAZAR. ... I just thought you were gonna be here for a while, ya know? I got Mets tickets, I fixed up my extra room, I bought sheets —

ROOFTOP. Why don't you come back to L.A. with me then? Yeah! ... B, I got a little spot in the Hills, jacuzzi. I'm goin' to a barbecue tomorrow night at Barry White's crib, man — Barry White — and believe me, when Barry hosts a get together, the brother throws down! You could come too, Flip — if ya want.

BALTHAZAR. I can't.

ROOFTOP. Well you should think on it. You been talkin' 'bout comin' out for a visit for years now. Lotta private security work out in L.A., man. Lotta rich mothahfuckahs who'd pay good money for a New York City detective to oversee their protection. You'd be clockin' ducats to get a suntan, man! You got a girlfriend, B?

BALTHAZAR. Nah.

ROOFTOP. How 'bout you, Flip?

FLIP. I'm married.

ROOFTOP. *(To Flip.)* God bless ya. *(To Balthazar.)* All I'm sayin', you divorced, you been a cop since you graduated high school, and — if I can speak frankly — you look about eighty-five years old, brother. The last jammy my man Barry threw — women outnumbered men ten to one, B, and dass all I'm gonna say about that!

BALTHAZAR. I'm goin' to the funeral — and you should too.

ROOFTOP. Would if I could —

BALTHAZAR. — It's fuckin' Sister Rose, man.

ROOFTOP. I'm done with funerals! Don't mind a wake, but fuck a funeral, man. Buried my pops, my little brother. My God, son — I was there for you on that, Balthazar. Right? Up on that hill, away from the crowd?

BALTHAZAR. Yeah.

ROOFTOP. ... All them crazy Dominicans on your ex-wife's side tryin' ta blame you, tryin' ta tear your ass in two? That one mothahfuckah wit' the stiletto? ... And your moms? ... Shit, they shouldn't make no kid-size caskets, oughta juss be one size fits all.

BALTHAZAR. Anyway. *(Beat. Rooftop drinks.)*

ROOFTOP. Damn, this is some lousy-ass cognac — they ain't got

39

no Henny up in here?

FLIP. Sold out.

ROOFTOP. This is some ridiculousness right here. The whole thing. Fuckin' cognac, fuckin' wake. Shit.

BALTHAZAR. Salut!

ROOFTOP. Salut. *(They drink. Silence.)*

FLIP. I was, I was thinkin' 'bout your brother's funeral before, Rooftop.

ROOFTOP. ... Lil' Chrissy.

BALTHAZAR. Chrissy was a good kid.

ROOFTOP. He was a dumb-ass kid is what he was! I mean, I know you was tight with him Flip, but, shit — how many kids fell down elevator shafts that summer — like, six?! Every other day on the Eyewitness News, Bill Buetel talkin' 'bout "another young boy falls to his death today" — wasn't like the word wasn't out! Stay away from the fuckin' elevator! But, nah, Chrissy always had to be nosy, adventurous —

BALTHAZAR. We were the same —

ROOFTOP. Balthazar, did you fall down an elevator shaft that summer?! Did Flip? Did I? Did any of Chrissy and Flip's crew? Chrissy didn't have no sense, and subsequently, he didn't have no eleventh birthday party neither!

FLIP. ... I juss ... I juss remember after the funeral, still being in my little suit, and walking over to that spot in the projects where me and Chrissy always used ta be at — and you two were there.

BALTHAZAR. *(To Rooftop.)* ... Drinkin' on some pink champale, remember?

FLIP. ... I remember seeing you, Rooftop, and you lookin' at me real hard — I thought you was gonna maybe hit me or chase me away — but then you just handed me the bottle and said, "Sip on this for Chrissy" — and, I, I had never tasted liquor before, but, I started to put the bottle to my lips anyway, and then you were like, "Got to spill a little on the ground first, kid." So I did, but I felt nervous because I had fucked up and I spilt a little bit of it on my pants and shoes. But then, I took my sip, and, I, I passed the bottle over to you, Balthazar, and then, I looked over at you, Rooftop, and, you, you came over to me and just gave me this hug, and I juss remember it felt real good, especially at that moment, 'cuz it was like you didn't hesitate, and ... and it just felt good, ya know?

ROOFTOP. Yeah. I know.

40

FLIP. I listen to you on the radio sometimes.

ROOFTOP. Ya do?

FLIP. You come on some satellite, computer thing that's hooked into my cable TV.

ROOFTOP. Where you live at?

FLIP. Wisconsin.

ROOFTOP. 'Cuz you know, they talkin' about takin' the show national.

BALTHAZAR. For real?

ROOFTOP. Yeah, brother. See, right now, we number three behind Steve Harvey and Large in Charge.

BALTHAZAR. Who's Large in Charge?

ROOFTOP. Some fat mothahfuckah thinks he's somebody 'cuz he's a fat motherfuckah — but he ain't got no game. All's he got is billboards. It's all about the billboards out there.

BALTHAZAR. You got a billboard?

ROOFTOP. Yeah. You wanna see a photo? *(Rooftop goes into his wallet.)*

BALTHAZAR. Oh, shit — looks who's here.

ROOFTOP. *(Reflexively.)* Inez?!

BALTHAZAR. Look — *(Father Lux motors towards the table.)*

ROOFTOP. Aw man, now what's all this about? *(Father Lux approaches.)*

FATHER LUX. *(To Flip and Balthazar.)* Hello ... *(To Rooftop.)* Didn't recognize you with the hat and glasses.

ROOFTOP. Tryin' ta keep it on the D.L., know what I'm sayin'?

FATHER LUX. Ah. You're hiding.

ROOFTOP. Not "hiding," juss not advertising.

FATHER LUX. Hiding.

ROOFTOP. You a funny cat, you know that?

FATHER LUX. If you're not hiding, take off the hat and glasses.

ROOFTOP. I am a grown man, Father — I believe I can attire myself as I please.

BALTHAZAR. You wanna drink, Father?

FATHER LUX. I want a dry Manhattan desperately — I plan to have three once I'm finished here.

ROOFTOP. Finished? Finished what?

FATHER LUX. Look you — Take off your hat and glasses.

ROOFTOP. Now, Father, you a father, and a war veteran, cut off at the knees and all, and you ain't a bad guy, but —

FATHER LUX. — Take off your hat and glasses or I'll turn

41

around and leave right now.

ROOFTOP. Yeah, well, forgive me Father — but that ain't much of a terrifying threat.

FATHER LUX. It's not? *(Beat. Rooftop takes off his shit.)*

ROOFTOP. ... You an annoying mothahfuckah, and I don't feel no guilt saying it.

FATHER LUX. Look at me.

ROOFTOP. What? *(Father Lux extends his hands.)*

FATHER LUX. I want you to pray with me. Will you pray with me?

ROOFTOP. Pray?! Goddamnit, father — this is a bar — ain't no tabernacle!

FATHER LUX. You don't think God is here now?

ROOFTOP. I don't know.

FATHER LUX. God spends a lot more time here than he does next door.

ROOFTOP. Yeah, well, that explains a lot!

FATHER LUX. Take my hands now. Pray with me.

ROOFTOP. C'mon man! — I'm here with my peeps, took the damn red-eye, no sleep —

FATHER LUX. — Say the Lord's Prayer with me. Would you do that?

ROOFTOP. For what?

FATHER LUX. Would you say the Lord's Prayer with me? Then, I'll go. *(Beat. Rooftop takes Father's hands.)*

ROOFTOP. You a pest, Lux. Fuckin' pesty.

FATHER LUX. ... OK ... Ready?

ROOFTOP. ... How's that go again?

FATHER LUX. "Our father" —

ROOFTOP. Right, yeah, of course.

FATHER LUX. *(To Balthazar.)* Care to join?

BALTHAZAR. Sorry Father — I don't do that no more.

FATHER LUX. *(To Flip.)* How about you?

FLIP. You don't mind?

FATHER LUX. Come on, son ... OK ... Let's speak it silently, but together, and with care.

ROOFTOP. Right. Let's roll. *(They pray the Lord's Prayer silently. Balthazar takes this all in. A beat. Rooftop and Father Lux regard each other.)*

FATHER LUX. I saw your ex-wife.

ROOFTOP. Inez?!

FATHER LUX. I mean, that's what this is all about, isn't it?

ROOFTOP. Where'd you see Inez at?

FATHER LUX. Is Inez what this is all about?

ROOFTOP. You didn't speak to her, did you?!

FATHER LUX. No.

ROOFTOP. Don't lie.

FATHER LUX. What made you decide to come to confession today?

ROOFTOP. Hold up! What was she doin' when ya saw her?

FATHER LUX. Talking on her cell phone.

ROOFTOP. And how'd you know it was her?

FATHER LUX. Because it was her.

ROOFTOP. She had on that dark red dress?

FATHER LUX. Ah. You saw her too.

ROOFTOP. ... So?!

FATHER LUX. So, did you see her before or after you were suddenly overcome — after thirty years — with the desire for spiritual absolution?

ROOFTOP. Now dass — dass private!

BALTHAZAR. Take a walk, Flip?

FLIP. Sure. *(Balthazar and Flip begin rising.)*

FATHER LUX. No. Stay ... *(To Rooftop.)* I will not leave without an answer.

ROOFTOP. Nah, man. Nah. *(Beat.)*

FATHER LUX. *(To rooftop.)* I'm not a good priest. I don't visit the sick because I'm afraid to go outside in my vestments. They don't let me say mass anymore. I haven't left the rectory next door since I was transferred here nine months ago. And, I don't want to. Black people scare me. I don't particularly like them. Or you, really. Most of the time, I don't believe in God at all, and when I do — I'm furious at him ... That's as honest as I can be.

ROOFTOP. ... I seen her before I came to see ya ... She didn't see me, but I saw her. After she turned the corner, I opened up the car door and I vomited everything I had inside me onto the sidewalk — and I mean everything. My kidneys were flappin' against my ribs. My heart was pullin' against my chest. I tried to keep blowin' till my soul came up — just ta see if I still had one, but ... nothing came up, Father — nothin'. Just air ...

FATHER LUX. I can fix that.

ROOFTOP. C'mon man, you a old, racist, tired, mothahfuckin' peg-leg mothahfuckah, you can't fix nothing.

FATHER LUX. If you really believed that, you wouldn't be sitting here. And you wouldn't have walked into my confessional this morning.

ROOFTOP. But, Father ...

FATHER LUX. Tell me everything you've ever done in your entire life that you feel killed your soul.

ROOFTOP. But that'll take days!

FATHER LUX. I don't have a problem with that. Do you?

Scene 2

The bar and grill, two A.M. Marcia sits alone at a table. Gail, also alone, is vaguely visible at the bar. Quiet. Edwin storms in upset, sees Marcia, looks for a seat as far from her as possible.

MARCIA. Is there something going on out there I should know about?

EDWIN. What?!

MARCIA. I said: Is there something going on out there that I should know about?

EDWIN. That you should know about? — no.

MARCIA. But, there's something going on out there?

EDWIN. What?!

MARCIA. I said: But there's something going on out there?

EDWIN. Going on out where?

MARCIA. Out there! Is there something going on out there?!

EDWIN. What are you yellin' about?! No! There is nothing going on out there!

MARCIA. I'm sorry, OK? It's just, the way you barged in, I thought, maybe —

EDWIN. Well, you thought incorrect, OK?!

MARCIA. ... Yeah, screw you too.

EDWIN. Excuse me?!

MARCIA. I said: Blow it out your ass and dry up! Oaf!

EDWIN. Look! The best thing you should do right now would be to refrain your ass!

MARCIA. Refrain my ass?! Refrain my ass from what?!

EDWIN. Juss shut it off, OK?! Shut it up and shut it off!

MARCIA. ... Jackass.

EDWIN. Ya know — there's a word for you!

44

MARCIA. There's lots of words for you — why don't you go buy a children's book and learn some?!

EDWIN. You know what — *(Pinky enters.)*

PINKY. — Hi Edwin!

EDWIN. Pinky! Jesus Christ, where in the hell you been at, Pinky?! Huh?! ... No! No, do not come closer! Do not come closer, Pinky, 'cuz I'm liable to take off my belt right here in this bar!

PINKY. Why?

EDWIN. Where the fuck you been?!

PINKY. Out?

EDWIN. What time I sent you out for Yodels, Pinky?

PINKY. Um ... Before noon?

EDWIN. Goddamn right it was before noon! Ten-thirty in the morning! Ten-thirty in the morning I sent you out for Yodels and milk — what time is it now?!

PINKY. Late?

EDWIN. Pinky!

PINKY. Very late?

EDWIN. Two in the morning, Pinky! It's two in the fuckin' morning!

PINKY. I'm sorry —

EDWIN. Fuck you "I'm sorry" — where's the bodega from here?

PINKY. Up the block.

EDWIN. So then how in the fuck did it take you sixteen hours to walk up the fuckin' block?! Answer me!

PINKY. I'm sorry.

EDWIN. I called the police! The fire department! The fuckin' neighbors! *(Pinky tries to hand Edwin a smushed Yodel.)*

PINKY. I, I saved you a Yodel! *(Edwin slaps it out of his hand violently.)*

EDWIN. Where you been at? Answer me!

PINKY. That hurt, Edwin.

EDWIN. I'm gonna call up Social Services, Pinky!

PINKY. No!

EDWIN. Yes I am!

PINKY. I was with Norca, OK?!

EDWIN. Stop lying!

PINKY. I'm not lying, I was with Norca! *(Edwin takes out his cell phone.)*

EDWIN. I'm dialing the number, Pinky!

PINKY. I was with Norca, I swear! I saw her by the corner and I said, "Hi Norca," and she said, "Fuck off, Retardo" (like how she calls me), but then I gave her some Yodels, and the milk, and the change, and I told her about my disability check, and we cashed it at the pharmacy, and we went to her friend to buy marijuana, and we went to a bar, and she smoked marijuana and drank margaritas and I smoked three cigarettes and ate a cheeseburger and drank a lot of Sprite, and nobody looked at me funny, and we talked, and that's truth, Edwin, I swear!

EDWIN. That fucking bitch!

PINKY. You're not gonna call Social Services are you?

EDWIN. Pinky: this story? It's a true one?

PINKY. It's true, Edwin — it's the best time I ever had in my life!

EDWIN. "Best time you ever had"?! That miserable bitch! Let Norca take care of your ass 24-7-365, see how many best times you have then!

PINKY. I know.

EDWIN. No you don't know — you don't know shit.

PINKY. We talked so much, Edwin. You wouldn't believe what we talked about. She said I was her best friend! She said I was the smartest person she ever met!

EDWIN. Yeah — you so smart you let that fuckin' bitch call you a retart, steal your money, and cash your fuckin' check. Real smart, Pinky.

PINKY. Can I have a hug, Edwin?

EDWIN. Did I tell you stay away from Norca?

PINKY. You tol' me Norca didn't like me, but you were wrong.

EDWIN. I was wrong?!

PINKY. I'm sorry —

EDWIN. No, Pinky, you said it, live with it.

PINKY. I didn't mean it.

EDWIN. Go home, Pinky!

PINKY. But I wanna stay with you!

EDWIN. Well I don't wanna stay with you! How's that?! How's that, Pinky?! Don't you understand that I have to know where you are?! That every minute of every day I have to be able to know that you're not dead somewhere?! But I guess I'm "wrong" about that too! "Wrong" about a lot of things!

PINKY. No.

EDWIN. Guess I was wrong going to court to keep you after Mom died, wrong to stay in this neighborhood where you feel familiar, wrong to tell Social Services to go fuck themselves, guess I was wrong every toy, every game, every movie, every dinner, every weekend, every night a my whole fuckin' life!

PINKY. No.

EDWIN. And that today, Pinky — out of all the fuckin' days in the year — with everything going on here — that you got to pick today to spazz out and terrify me and let me down when I needed you — for once — to be a little less a retart and a little more a fuckin' man — I will never forgive you for that ... Never ... Yeah, dass right, cry! You gave me six heart attacks today — you should cry! Now go the fuck home, you little fuckin' baby — and pack your fuckin' bags! Go! *(Pinky exits. Beat. Edwin takes out his cell.)* Mrs. McNulty? Mrs. McNulty, this is Edwin the Super, sorry to call so late ... No, I'm fine. Pinky, he's comin' up the block now, could you wait for him by the lamppost? Yeah. Yeah, thanks. Nah, let him watch TV, whatever he wants. Thanks. You too, dear. *(Edwin hangs up, finds a seat, his head collapsing into his arms. He heaves. Silence. Marcia looks at Edwin. Silence. Marcia finds tissues in her purse, crosses to Edwin, leaves tissues on table, goes back to her seat. Silence. Marcia considers, then picks up her food, drink, silverware, napkin, and purse, crosses to Edwin's table. Sits. Silence.)*

MARCIA. My grandfather was an alcoholic ... He used to beat up my grandmother, and my mom, and Sister Rose ... When Sister Rose was eleven, she stood up to my grandfather, and after that, he would only beat her ... The result of this is that my mom and Sister Rose both grew up to become different kinds of maniacs ... They were both alcoholics ... They're both dead ... And I'm just like both of them ... And I think maybe you are too.

EDWIN. ... I, uh ... You gonna eat that?

MARCIA. Uh, no.

EDWIN. Mind if I do?

MARCIA. Please.

EDWIN. I always get hungry ... when I have a lot a feelings.

MARCIA. I understand.

EDWIN. I, personally, don't think I'm a maniac, and — lemme finish — I think that although you're a little ... unique — I don't think you're that either.

MARCIA. Not yet, but maybe soon.

EDWIN. And I don't think Sister Rose was a maniac neither.

MARCIA. Well, that's where you're wrong.

EDWIN. Lemme tell you something: You know who taught me how ta ride a bike? Sister Rose. You know who told me I was handsome all the time till I started believin' it? Sister Rose. Who helped my brother Pinky learn stuff every day after school so he wouldn't get sent to a special school someplace else? Sister Rose.

MARCIA. But that's —

EDWIN. — Hold up. Yes, she could be wild, mean sometimes, she had a big stick and she knew howta use it, believe me, but, ask any kid who grew 'round a hundred twenty-first, and if they're being honest? They'll tell ya something special she done for them ... 'cuz ... dass who she was ... and dass why so many people are turnin' up outta the woodwork here, 'cuz in their heart? — they know ... They know she was ... that She was Our Lady, ya know?

MARCIA. I wish my mom could hear you talking about her sister like that.

EDWIN. Yeah, well, I wish a lot a things too.

MARCIA. Like what?

EDWIN. ... I dunno.

MARCIA. What?

EDWIN. Nothing. Just ...

MARCIA. What?

EDWIN. You're very pretty, Marcia. I just think you're so ... pretty ...

MARCIA. ...

GAIL. Sorry to bother you, but ... Question: Do I seem gay to you?

MARCIA. ... "Seem"?

GAIL. OK ... Do I seem very gay?

EDWIN. No, I wouldn't say that you seemed "very" gay.

MARCIA. Edwin, be honest.

EDWIN. You seem quite gay.

MARCIA. Just "quite"?

GAIL. *(To Marcia.)* So, you're saying what? I seem "very quite" gay?

MARCIA. Well, I would have to say, I mean, if you really wanna know, that you appear to be exceedingly gay.

EDWIN. No, I disagree.

MARCIA. Edwin, the man is gay!

GAIL. But if I was dressed differently —

MARCIA. Still gay.

GAIL. If I had a complete makeover —

MARCIA. Completely made-over gay.

GAIL. So you're saying, even if I change everything about me, and I mean everything —

MARCIA. Well, I'd have to see it first, but ...

GAIL. Thank you for your honesty. *(Gail goes back to his drink.)*

MARCIA. Would you ever consider shaving your moustache?

EDWIN. My moustache? I don't think so.

MARCIA. That's OK. Would you like to have dinner with me tomorrow ... or breakfast?

EDWIN. ... I can't.

MARCIA. Why not?

EDWIN. Funeral.

MARCIA. I mean after the funeral.

EDWIN. I got stuff.

MARCIA. Well, how 'bout the next day?

EDWIN. Workin'.

MARCIA. Call in sick.

EDWIN. Don't you take no for an answer?

MARCIA. Why should I?

EDWIN. C'mon. You saw.

MARCIA. Saw what?

EDWIN. My brother.

MARCIA. So?!

EDWIN. So, you wanna love me? Decide to love me right now? Marry me tomorrow? Move in with me and my brother? Love him too? Stay here in this neighborhood for as long as it takes? You wanna do that, I'll give it a shot.

MARCIA. ... That is so unfair.

EDWIN. Welcome to my life that ain't gonna change. *(Edwin goes to exit.)*

MARCIA. ... Martyr!

EDWIN. My brother needs me!

MARCIA. You need your brother! God, haven't you ever heard of therapy?!

EDWIN. I choose loyalty!

MARCIA. Yeah, well what good does that do me?! *(Beat.)*

EDWIN. Look, Marcia, it's just better this way. *(Edwin exits. Silence.)*

GAIL. "When I became a man, I put away childish things" —

MARCIA. What?

GAIL. He should read Corinthians.

MARCIA. What?

GAIL. "When I became a man, I put away childish things" — Saint Paul.

MARCIA. ... Fuck off! *(A long beat. Flip enters, drunk, but steady, approaches Gail, face to face. Beat.)*

GAIL. What? *(Flip kisses Gail.)* You kissed me. *(Flip kisses Gail again.)* That's twice. You kissed me twice. In relative public, Robert.

FLIP. Damn straight.

GAIL. *(Re: Marcia.)* Right in front of that woman.

FLIP. Dass right. Can we go back to the hotel now? *(Beat.)*

GAIL. Do you know her?

FLIP. Who?

GAIL. That woman over there. Do you know her?

FLIP. ... Do I know her? Yeah. Yeah, I know her. Her name's Katie.

GAIL. ... Katie?

FLIP. Yeah. Katie Ryan. We were in the fifth grade together. Let's go.

GAIL. ... Katie Ryan?

FLIP. ... What?

GAIL. Katie Ryan, Robert? *(Beat.)*

FLIP. ... Don't ruin it, Gail.

GAIL. ... You don't really think I'm a bad actor, do you, Robert?

FLIP. You're ... my star.

GAIL. ... I'll send for my things. *(Gail goes to exit.)*

FLIP. "Send for your things"? —

GAIL. I'm thirty-seven years old, Robert ... Thirty-seven. And so are you.

FLIP. Gail?

GAIL. Thirty-seven. *(Gail exits.)*

Scene 3

Main viewing room. Five A.M. Vic is asleep. Edwin is asleep. Rooftop sits between them. Sonia sits alone. Inez reads her Bible.

ROOFTOP. ... Nezzie?

INEZ. ... Hello Walter.

ROOFTOP. Didn't see you come in.

INEZ. You was sleepin'.

ROOFTOP. What time is it, Nezzie?

INEZ. Dass not a watch on your wrist?

ROOFTOP. Right. Yeah ... Damn, five A.M. I gotta make a call. Gotta call in sick on my show this morning. You ever heard my show?

INEZ. Pay phone's just around the corner.

ROOFTOP. Anything happen while —

INEZ. — No.

ROOFTOP. Well, "no news is good news," right?

INEZ. What?

ROOFTOP. Well, I guess not in this case, huh? ... Reading your Bible I see.

INEZ. Trying to.

ROOFTOP. "Into the valley of the dead rode the six hundred"!

INEZ. Thass not the Bible, Walter.

ROOFTOP. Oh ... Say, I been to the church today.

INEZ. Yeah?

ROOFTOP. Went to confession.

INEZ. That musta took a while.

ROOFTOP. You have no idea. Father Lux, know him?

INEZ. I don't attend this parish anymore.

ROOFTOP. He the priest in the wheelchair.

INEZ. Oh him. Poor man. I saw him on the street, didn't see his collar — almost handed him a dollar.

ROOFTOP. Yeah, he ain't dapper like Father C was, but, he alright.

INEZ. Well, it sounds like it went well.

ROOFTOP. It did ... Say, Nezzie, you wanna take a little walk with me, maybe juss up to Cherry Park?

INEZ. No.

ROOFTOP. Why not?

INEZ. I don't think my husband would appreciate it for one thing.

ROOFTOP. Well how 'bout you, Nezzie — would you appreciate it?

INEZ. Look, my life is good, Walter. Got a good job, good husband, good life. I go to events, I do things, see things, I take a vacation every year — Hawaii. Trinidad. Wherevah I wanna go.

ROOFTOP. Where your husband at?

INEZ. He at home, Walter. You've heard of home, right? It's that place husbands hang out at sometimes? *(Gail enters with suitcase and newspaper. Rooftop and Inez glare at each other.)*

GAIL. Is this seat available?

SONIA. Oh. Yes. Sure.

GAIL. Thank you. *(To Inez.)* Hello.

INEZ. Goliath, right?

GAIL. Actually, it's Gail. Gail Saunders.

INEZ. OK.

GAIL. How are you?

INEZ. Hanging in.

GAIL. *(To Inez.)* ... I quit drinking today. Today is day one.

INEZ. Well, congratulations.

GAIL. I'm not an alcoholic, but, sometimes I drink all day and into the night. *(To Rooftop.)* I'm Gail. Gail Saunders.

ROOFTOP. I seen you at the bar I think.

GAIL. You're "Up on the roof with Rooftop," right?

ROOFTOP. Yes. Yes I am.

GAIL. I'm a fan of your show, I'm a listener.

ROOFTOP. Thank you.

GAIL. How are you?

ROOFTOP. I'm fine, how are you?

GAIL. Gay. I'm gay.

ROOFTOP. That right?

SONIA. My cousin's gay.

GAIL. Is he available? — just kidding. *(To Rooftop.)* Anyway, I'm homosexual.

ROOFTOP. Well, glad ta know ya.

GAIL. And I'm an actor.

ROOFTOP. Alright.

GAIL. See? I bought *Backstage* — it's a publication that lists auditions.

ROOFTOP. OK.

GAIL. Auditions for actors: gay and straight.

ROOFTOP. Right.

GAIL. Me, of course, being gay.

ROOFTOP. OK, now, is there something about me that suggests to you that all this might be of some kinda particular interest to me?

INEZ. Walter.

ROOFTOP. There's a room full of people here — why he gotta be directing all his little facts at me, Nezzie?

INEZ. Quit callin' me "Nezzie" — like you on some kinda intimate terms!

ROOFTOP. I am on intimate terms!

INEZ. No you're not! You're on "Fuck you" terms, Walter — so go slink off in your fuckin' limo back to La-La land, or wherever it is you con people into payin' you good money for nonsense, and leave me out of it!

ROOFTOP. You tryin' ta tell me you can't pretend to read a Bible someplace else?!

INEZ. What?!

52

ROOFTOP. You heard me! It's five A.M. in the morning, you got a so-called husband at home, and there ain't gonna be no goddamned wake, so why in hell you still here, Nezzie Thompson?!

INEZ. You better get out of here, Walter!

ROOFTOP. Nezzie —

INEZ. No way — Fuck you! You think 'cuz you went to a church and hustled some bummy old priest that it gives you the right to come to me any way you want?! You killed my heart, Walter! Killed it! You don't remember Sister Rose talkin' 'bout "every woman has a secret garden"?! Well, you took my secret garden and dropped a fuckin' atomic bomb on it and now it's just scorched earth and ashes — burnt-up dirt.

ROOFTOP. You talkin' fifteen years now!

INEZ. Fifteen years, five hundred years! That's who I am! You knew that from jump! You knew it! Did ya not know it, Walter? Look me in my eye and say you didn't an' I'll give you the Academy Award for Best Stone Cold Liar of the fuckin' millennium! You think I'm upset?! You should meet my husband — the damn fool fell in love with a woman got a bombed-out graveyard for a mothahfuckin' heart! And he's a good man, Walter — good and decent and loyal and nuthin' like you, so ... OK?! And I'm doin' it to him like you did it to me, so, can you just get up off me now?! *(Rooftop rises.)*

ROOFTOP. Fine! I'll respect your wishes!

INEZ. You don't know a damn thing about "respect."

ROOFTOP. I need to make my phone call anyway!

INEZ. Yeah, be sure to call someone who gives a shit. *(Rooftop crosses to exit.)*

ROOFTOP. *(To Gail.)* You caused this!

GAIL. I'm very sorry.

ROOFTOP. You wanna tell somebody you gay, tell Oprah, mothahfuckah! *(Rooftop exits.)*

EDWIN. *(Waking up.)* What time is it?

SONIA. Five.

EDWIN. In the morning?

SONIA. Yeah.

EDWIN. *(To Inez.)* They find Sister Rose?

INEZ. No.

EDWIN. No one heard from Balthazar?

INEZ. No.

EDWIN. Sumpthin' happen, Inez?

INEZ. Go back to sleep, baby.

GAIL. *(To Edwin.)* Hi.

EDWIN. Oh yeah. Hi.

GAIL. I heard you mention in the bar that you were a Super? I'm wondering: any apartments available?

EDWIN. Not at this time.

GAIL. Do you know where I can get an apartment for four hundred dollars a month?

EDWIN. I dunno — Delaware?

GAIL. New York's expensive, huh?

EDWIN. Try Queens.

GAIL. They film *Law and Order* here in New York, don't they?

EDWIN. I don't know that information ... Inez, Could you wake me if something happens?

INEZ. Yeah, Eddy. *(Edwin goes back to sleep.)*

GAIL. *(To Sonia.)* I'm planning to try out for *Law and Order*.

SONIA. You're an actor?

GAIL. I am.

SONIA. My cousin's an actor.

GAIL. The gay one?

SONIA. No. It's a different cousin. But he's an actor.

GAIL. Small world.

SONIA. ... He was on *Law and Order*.

GAIL. Really?

SONIA. ... Well, his back was — but you could definitely tell it was him — I mean, if you knew him.

GAIL. Oh.

SONIA. ... He had a line. He pointed to a pot of coffee and said; "There."

INEZ. *(To Sonia.)* Excuse me, but, why are you here? Do you know somebody here? Did ya go to school here? What?

SONIA. My friend Marcia — she was Sister Rose's niece.

INEZ. An' where's this Marcia at?

SONIA. She left.

INEZ. And you're still here because?

SONIA. ... I guess I'll go then. *(As Sonia goes to exit, Rooftop re-emerges in the doorway.)*

ROOFTOP. I'm a make this call 'cuz I have to, but I need you to think on this till I get back: Ain't my fault about your husband, dass on you. And it ain't my fault 'bout your scorched-up heart — you married me juss like I married you. And I got no choice but to try and forgive myself for everything I done to you, 'cuz, what's the fuckin'

alternative, Inez? I usta think there was some other option, some way 'round it, but there really ain't. I can try an' forgive myself, or, I can go jump off the GW — and dass it! I feel guilty 'bout a girl been dead fifteen years, and you? You angry at a boy — a boy, Inez — not me … Do I wish I had done it different back then? Hell yeah. Even now, I'm tempted to take this conversation in another direction jus so I could get with you. And I could get with you if I worked my game right, don't tell me I couldn't 'cuz I'm a fuckin' professional — but what would be the point a that? I lost you — dass my cross. 'Cuz you was my royal. And I killed it. But if you wanna walk around all these years later still tryin' ta play dead, dass your waste, not mine … dass on you. I'm a make my call now. *(Rooftop exits. Pause.)*
GAIL. I know I don't know you, but I would just like to say —
INEZ. — Would you put me in a cab, please?
GAIL. Yes. I'll leave with you. *(Gail gathers his things, escorts Inez out.)*
SONIA. … Bye. *(Sonia sits alone with the sleeping men. Pause. Balthazar enters, dishevelled, holding a brown paper bag.)*
BALTHAZAR. *(To Sonia.)* Who are you?
SONIA. Sonia?
BALTHAZAR. Sonia who?
SONIA. You're very drunk.
BALTHAZAR. Days like these, Sonia, it's very important to be sober as a judge or just blind drunk — I chose the latter.
SONIA. Oh.
BALTHAZAR. You remember that, Sonia.
SONIA. OK.
BALTHAZAR. Good. Now, pa fuera.
SONIA. Pa fuera?
BALTHAZAR. Goodbye. Go. Now.
SONIA. Um —
BALTHAZAR. — Now! *(Sonia exits. Balthazar pokes Vic.)* Hey wake up.
VIC. What time is it?
BALTHAZAR. Sssh. I don't know. Don't wake him up.
VIC. They said you weren't comin' back.
BALTHAZAR. Well, that's 'cuz they know me, Rick.
VIC. Vic.
BALTHAZAR. Vic. Yes, of course. Sorry, Vic.
VIC. So what's the word?
BALTHAZAR. … Here.
VIC. What's this?

BALTHAZAR. Your pants. Wallet's gone, but ...

VIC. Where'd they find my pants?

BALTHAZAR. By the river. Off the West Side Highway.

VIC. And what about Rose?

BALTHAZAR. The thing is —

VIC. What about Rose?!

BALTHAZAR. ... A coupla patrolmen, Vic, they found a large suitcase.

VIC. Suitcase?

BALTHAZAR. Yeah ... They found half of her, Vic.

VIC. Half?

BALTHAZAR. They're comin' for the casket now. We're gonna bury that part of her at eleven.

VIC. Half?

BALTHAZAR. Why donchu siddown?

VIC. I don't wanna siddown. Whaddya mean, "half"?!

BALTHAZAR. Vic —

VIC. "Half"?! Where's the other half?!

BALTHAZAR. We think prolly the river.

VIC. The river?! What's she doin' in the river?!

BALTHAZAR. Vic, she's not doing anything in the river. She's gone. She was gone before any of this happened.

VIC. So that means this is all OK?!

BALTHAZAR. It's not OK.

VIC. Then go back out there and find her! *(Pause.)*

BALTHAZAR. ... Vic.

VIC. Jesus!

BALTHAZAR. ... I know.

VIC. Jesus H. Christ! *(Vic sits, turning his back to Balthazar. Silence.)*

BALTHAZAR. ... Vic?

VIC. What?

BALTHAZAR. Here. That's for you. *(Balthazar hands Vic a small rosary. Vic examines it.)*

VIC. Was this...?

BALTHAZAR. No. It belonged to my son.

VIC. Your son?

BALTHAZAR. First Communion ... Remember the guy with the ham sandwiches?

VIC. Yeah?

BALTHAZAR. I'm the guy with the Ham sandwiches, Vic.

VIC. You?

BALTHAZAR. ... The morning my son disappeared? I had a hangover that morning. I let my seven-year-old boy go out and play ... alone. That's the truth, Vic.

VIC. Geez.

BALTHAZAR. My son adored Sister Rose. I want you to know that. Adored her. Just like you.

VIC. Yeah?

BALTHAZAR. Couldn't get enough of her. "Sister Rose this," "Sister Rose, that" — and she, I could see that she took a real interest in him — sincere — he was a real smart kid, my boy, ninety-eighth percentile.

VIC. That's, uh, that's good.

BALTHAZAR. First parent/teacher meeting I ever went to, Sister Rose told me my Juan Jose was special. "Not bright ... gifted."

VIC. Well she knew kids, dass for sure.

BALTHAZAR. ... I miss him a lot, Vic. *(Pause.)*

VIC. *(Re: the rosary.)* Look, I, I can't accept this —

BALTHAZAR. When my son was a baby, Vic —

VIC. — Yeah?

BALTHAZAR. I was, I was doing undercover "buy and busts" at the time. I was a big deal back then.

VIC. Yeah?

BALTHAZAR. Anyway, I would get home 'round six A.M., and I usta like to take him out of his crib onto the fire escape. I'd sit on a milk crate with a little pillow on it, maybe a beer, and I'd just hold him, ya know — hold him like, like this. You got kids, Vic?

VIC. Nieces and nephews.

BALTHAZAR. Well this one morning, it's breezy, right, nice breeze, and I'm spacing out, staring over at New Jersey, lost, and all the sudden I'm aware that he's stirring. So I look over my shoulder, and my boy, he's, he's feeling the breeze on him, and his face looks all puzzled — like he doesn't understand, right? — and his little hands, Vic, they're doing this ... *(Balthazar mimes his baby trying to catch the wind.)* He was trying, you know, my boy was trying to catch the wind, Vic ... I always remember that.

VIC. ... I bet that helps.

BALTHAZAR. It hurts, Vic ... It hurts a lot. *(Beat. Rooftop enters, but Inez is gone. Vic and Balthazar sit silently. Edwin is still sleeping on the bench. Blackout.)*

End of Play

PROPERTY LIST

Empty casket
Half-pint liquor bottle (BALTHAZAR)
Flask (FLIP)
Cigarette (PINKY)
Twenty-dollar bill (EDWIN)
Bag (MARCIA)
Inhaler (MARCIA)
Ketchup bottle (INEZ)
Joint (ROOFTOP)
Grocery bag (PINKY)
Fifty-dollar bill (ROOFTOP)
Mixed nuts (PINKY)
Drinks (BALTHAZAR, ROOFTOP, FLIP, MARCIA, GAIL)
Wallet (ROOFTOP)
Motorized wheelchair (FATHER LUX)
Yodel (PINKY)
Cell phone (EDWIN)
Tissues (MARCIA)
Food, silverware, napkin (MARCIA)
Bible (INEZ)
Suitcase (GAIL)
Newspaper (GAIL)
Brown paper bag (BALTHAZAR)
Rosary (BALTHAZAR)

SOUND EFFECTS

Loud knocking